Chokecherry

Chokecherry

Cover design and layout by Catherine Weiss.

Edited by Story Boyle, Jillian Boger, and Josh Savory.

Formatted by Josh Savory.

GAME
OVER
BOOKS

Game Over Books
www.gameoverbooks.com

Table of Contents

"Outside
the joy is clamoring. It is almost like the worst day of your life

is ordinary for everyone else."

—Ruth Awad, *In the gloaming, in the roiling night*

XX

I was twenty years old at a long glass table writing the same letter for a year. No. Let me start again. I was twenty years old taking photos of the sunset from the interior. "Black Velvet" slipped out of the jukebox before I tried to slip into the bar. I was twenty years old with dormant daddy issues. My lungs were coated in horseradish. The oven door was loose. The doctors never believed me. I was twenty years old and the college freshman mistook me for the next decade. Typical. I was twenty years old with aloe vera under my eyes. I kept forgetting to replace the batteries in my vibrator. None of my dates ever touched me. I was twenty years old and I never let any of my dates touch me. Wait. I was twenty years old, afraid I would die before the bars actually welcomed me and my dry tastes. I was twenty years old and always good company. I was twenty years old, my wisdom teeth tucked into the far end of my pillowcase. I was twenty years old and the last time I spoke to my father was in a diner the week before Christmas. I was twenty years old and then I wasn't. I was twenty-one years old, openly weeping while standing on black ice, grenadine on my teeth and winter sweat pooling in my party dress. The Roman numerals are getting less and less lonely, my handwriting shakier and shakier. My jaw padlocks itself every morning. I wonder: when the house plant loses a leaf, when the hive begins to crystallize in the sun, when the radio goes hungry—does it remember the way I do?

CHOKECHERRY

I imagine my uncle and grandfather's last moments.
    My own hands a triangle around my neck. My thumbs
just barely touch. I am hardy, like an oak

    fighting a chainsaw. I cough sap into the sink,
        and the porch light goes out. When I was thirteen,
I spent three months trying to get bathwater out
of my nose. My blue socks sticky on the tile floor. The nurse
        asked me what was on my mind, but I turned
the Walkman's volume up to its maximum. I'm almost twenty-two

now, and stumbling over my own memory like deforestation.
What have I lost? My wallet. Four wisdom teeth. I had a roommate
        who stole all my silverware. My parents' wedding cake
        is rotting in the freezer. My grandfather's last words
to me are in a stranger's handwriting. I guess I'll just say it:

my uncle broke his own neck while I was on my tiptoes
        trying to hang a mirror up in my bedroom. Everything
        my grandfather ate for two months straight became liquid
        in his lungs. I am still as tall as I was at ten. I need
to get a new inhaler. The nurse asks if I'm a smoker. No,
        but my parents are. No, but my best friends are.
        No, but when I was a kid we almost lost our house

in a wildfire. No, but choking to death seems to run
in the family. Sometimes I wake up gasping for air
        like my bed is on fire. Somewhere in Illinois,
there's a tree named after my uncle. It could be any tree,
though. How could I know which one? Would I see the smoke?

206 DAYS LATER

This time, there's no one around to call me back behind
the screen door—I wander to the bricks muddy
with my own handprints. The air is humid here;
I collect it in my hands. There's a fingerprint-shaped scar
on the nape of my neck that only I have touched. A crater
on the moon no one's landed on. There's a fountain
where I've only ever seen people stealing pennies
instead of offering them. I wish I could walk barefoot forever.
I wish I knew how to cartwheel.
Once, a girl I thought I would marry made a list
of all the people we had collectively lost in our lives:
let's name our children after them. I think I will always be
a slab of July cement, attracting only mosquitoes
and cherry syrup. I feel empty the way a museum
can be empty. I count my bones just to be sure,
as if a part of me takes off in the night while I sweat
myself to sleep.

(I take the pill with the cyclops' name)

I take the pill with the cyclops' name
and dance with the candle in my hands

until my ankles slip away from me.
On a notepad, I write: my limbs feel

like vegetables thrown around
at a farmers' market. I assume

that I assumed it would be important.
Earlier, I read the book about addiction

and told myself it was to understand
my parents, their parents, so on

until their last names dilute. In a hospital,
I once called the nurse carrying a balloon

of morphine to me beautiful. One fist
of wisdom teeth, another of hydrocodone.

The only alcohol I've ever known glowing
through me was as I tried to fall asleep

in a photo booth. I am only my parents
when I am in pain. I make sure that pain

is lonely. I toe the line while my useless
skeleton decides: never again. I dance

with the avalanche until I remember.

MAINE LAMENTS

Find me a fifth story window, and I will coax
a happier year out of the glass sheets before
midnight. From now on, my resolutions
won't be lobsters in a grocery store tank.
I boil the water for my bath instead. My skin
falters red, but not like delectable death,
more like the anatomy of a cautious optimism.
I'm thinking of my grandmother now,

and how when she was my age, she waitressed
in coastal Maine. Part of her job was to trek
into the front teeth of the Atlantic to catch
a lobster every time a rich man ordered one.
I'm thinking of my grandmother, and how manic
I was the last time we were in Maine together.
When I told her it hurt to stay still,
she said *let's run across this meadow*
as fast as we can. We both
wore dresses—I still remember

how the skirt billowed across my rushing
thighs, the switchgrass extending spindly fingers
to meet my legs. I'm thinking of how far my legs
have gotten me. I've run to the top floor
of a parking garage just to watch the sunset.
My knees are permanently embedded
with the imprints of dandelion stems. This year,
I want to slow-dance with all my best friends.
Wade in a hot spring. Learn how to climb a tree—
I want to stop being afraid of heights
that are of my own making.

PASSED LIGHT

In another life I'm a haberdasher. Bone splitter,
speaker of fluent Russian. In another life
I might have already died. The adults
told me: *you have been here before.* An old soul,

two knowing eyes. Too knowing. Once, my lips were chapped
beyond repair in Wyoming. Maybe it was Utah.
Sweat gluing blouse to body. Did I ever know
how to cock a pistol? I've always been afraid to, here.
Half my life ago, I woke up at 4:30 every morning

to make lunches for my sister and myself. I opened beer bottles
for my father with the chin of the coffee table. I rubbed
cornstarch into carpet so the house wouldn't smell
like my parents' throats. Stranger,
I've grown to resent the term *old soul.* It is this life
that made me know. It is this life that taught me
to be older than my body.

NOTNAME

From Wikipedia: "In art history, a Notname (or 'necessity-name')
is an invented name given to an artist whose identity has been lost."

I like to think that there's a universe
in which *Anonymous* is one person.

One time-traveling artist using
their two hands to create,

but never to name themselves,
paint pharaohs and princesses,

drain their signature of ink
and leaving only a memory. Then

it was not uncommon
to forget what your loved ones'

faces looked like after they died,
until they were just a name.

Is necessity not the act of naming?
There is a painting of Elizabeth I

as a teenager, her gown as red as her hair,
a small Bible in her suspicious hands.

The name of the artist is not known,
and this is what I know: I am from

a family of writers. Most of us
can barely draw a childlike sun,

or our own faces. I have an uncle
who has been dead nearly 10 years,

but I still remember what he looked like.
I have a recording of his voice

that I can play anytime I want.
There are days when I am still so sick

with grief that I almost want to forget
his name. I have never written

that fact until now, but look:
I have the ability. The words

to describe those spaces
still often escape me, and that's

when I wish I were a painter.
I have a theory that *Anonymous*

is a time-traveling artist,
leaves when whatever world

they're in starts crumbling. They have
no time for wars, or plagues, or an entire

country's mourning. They gain the love
of a sovereign, then they leave

to be as nameless and blank
as their first canvases again.

ELEGY ENDING IN MY GRANDMOTHER REMEMBERING

After George Abraham

After my grandfather's body is carried out,
the hospital bed becomes a museum artifact.
My mother runs outside towards the streetlights.

The hospital bed becomes a museum artifact;
my mother runs outside towards the streetlights.
Meanwhile, my grandmother searches for his watch.

My mother runs outside towards the streetlights.
Meanwhile, my grandmother searches for his watch.
Your grandfather will need this when he comes back, she tells me.

Meanwhile, my grandmother searches for his watch—
Your grandfather will need this when he comes back, she tells me—
& I quietly beg all the clocks to forget themselves too.

Your grandfather will need this when he comes back, she tells me,
& I quietly beg all the clocks to forget themselves too.
What a knife drawer of a word that's become: *forget*.

I quietly beg all the clocks to forget themselves too.
What a knife drawer of a word that's become—*forget*,
as if we haven't been trying to hide our unconscious wounds.

What a knife drawer of a word that's become: *forget*.
As if we haven't been trying to hide our unconscious wounds,
my mother & I try to smile before we cobble the obituary.

As if we haven't been trying to hide our unconscious wounds,
my mother & I try to smile before we cobble the obituary,
but again, my grandmother asks, & again, we quietly bleed.

My mother & I try to smile before we cobble the obituary,
but again, my grandmother asks, & again, we quietly bleed,
& I stain everything under the table with my confused grief.

Again, my grandmother asks, & again, we quietly bleed,
& I stain everything under the table with my confused grief.
The truth becomes sharper every time it's said aloud.

I stain everything under the table with my confused grief.
The truth becomes sharper every time it's said aloud,
& my grandmother buckles under its inevitable blade.

The truth becomes sharper every time it's said aloud.
My grandmother is buckling under inevitable blades—

BOOMTOWN
(ALL THE PLACES I AM NOT)

It's wildfire season, 9:30 and the sun still isn't setting. We always find ourselves waiting in the pink mansion by the tracks. Not pink like the sky, or love—pink like the skin on my shoulders right out of the shower. There's a blackberry bush near the porch that I still can't bring myself to steal from. My forehead is a ravine. I tell you, *I have been afraid my whole life. I've had the same nightmare about getting hit by a train for years. My shoes feel so uneasy here.* We go upstairs to sleep. We watch the sky shift dark again. You tell me, *you don't ever have to be brave for my sake.*

Those Georgia city lights in August—
they were not sweet. I searched
frantically for the hotel's rooftop door;
I wondered if I should be drunk.
This was my disco ball despair, and
Decatur was beckoning me to dance.

Perhaps that should have been
the night we met, but it wasn't.
You were wasted in the lobby;
I was manic on the roof. So manic,
death sounded like a party to me.
Years later, we laughed about it

together, and decided we were grateful
to have met under better circumstances.
Happier circumstances; sober circumstances.

I don't talk about the Romero fire,
how it was right in front of my
bedroom window, how I was 8,
how I didn't sleep at all that night,
how I didn't sleep at all for the next
10 years—

If I ever have children, I couldn't stand to give them my father's last name.
They should have my mother's name instead: they should be Wallaces,
cleaning fiddleheads and reading Rilke on the porch. If only *Havens* could be
a comfort to my children, and not a backdoor they'd have to split open.

I didn't know what a cicada was
until I was 9. I spent 2 weeks
in Urbana with my grandparents.
I learned how to play cribbage,
and who Jack Ruby was. I told
my grandmother, *I'm scared of*
the humming outside. I'm scared of

guns. She assured me cicadas
are harmless. They just think
their sheer wings, their woodwinds,
their party dresses, make beautiful
music. Still, I imagined: a man
with a gun killing a man who once had
a gun, again and again.

My mother was raised atheist,
but has spent so much of my life
explaining God to me. She believes
God can be anything, including nothing.
She says her only church was having
children. Everyday, she wears the same
silver medal under her clothes for Dymphna,
patron saint of the mentally ill
and runaways.

Maybe this is my religion:
self-awareness and wary survival.

When we were reintroduced, you
remembered me from before:
how I spoke as if I had more to say,
but refused to. That night, I think I said
more than I had in 6 months. I reeled

in it—the confusing easiness.
The week after we both went home,
cartography splintered again, I texted:

I miss your voice.

When he was young, my father tried
to run down a cop who had pulled him over.

A man's hand once swallowed my entire shoulder
at a house show; I threatened to slice it off.

Will I ever relearn how to drive?
Have I lost my religion? Did we run out
of flour? Will we become our fathers?
How do I comb the tangles out of
my hair? How do I get the blood stain
out of my favorite bra? Can you teach me
how to read the atlas? Does the honey
ever go bad? If I ever become my father,
will I still love you? Do you know?
Will I stop waking up with headaches
someday? Do you know?

Men ruin everything with their danger.

I say, *I don't think I'll stay in Idaho.*

I say, *I don't know when Arizona
will stop hurting.*

I say, *I love you.*

I say, *I don't know if I love you
enough to live in Minnesota.*

I say, *Illinois is an obituary.*

I say, *I still think Georgia
wants me dead.*

I say, *I don't have a passport.*

I say, *Another state exists*
in my head. You are its capital.

My ideal life:

We own a house that soaks its insides in natural light every day. I breathe
easy in the summer. You start writing again. I learn how to cook Julia Child's
beef bourguignon flawlessly. We always manage to get enough sleep. I take
you to Maine, where my grandmother was raised to raise potatoes and I
spent 10 of my summers eating Grape-Nuts ice cream and rereading every
book in the farmhouse.

I tell you the story of the July my family's flight was cancelled, and we ended
up deserted in JFK. Of driving from Queens to Cornville. Of my mother
almost throwing the map out the window in Connecticut. Of my father,
yelling and yelling and yelling. Of my mother trying to get out of the car
in the middle of the highway on the coastline of Maine. Of me screaming:
don't leave us with him.

I tell you this story, and I am able to laugh.

What exactly led me to Idaho—

the escapism? The deliverance?
The living room floor where
someone wrote *PUNK DOVE*
on my knuckles in Sharpie,
and told me I didn't have
to ever go back to Tucson
if I didn't want to? The way
"This Must Be The Place"
sounded less heartbroken coming

from a different city's speakers?
I lived in a motel for two weeks.
I almost froze to death next
to the radiator my landlord promised
actually worked. I cried
on the kitchen floor every day
for a whole season. And yes,
I would do it all again.

I plan on eventually turning into a plague
for hurtful men to avoid. I fantasize
about my knuckles turning into locusts,
each one reproducing by the nanosecond.

With the humidifier on, my grandmother
pressed a ginger root into my palm.
It calms the nerves. Her Illinois kitchen
was a blue I wanted to swallow. Cobalt.
Van Gogh. Ishtar. I'm still worried
all the time, but the heat on my teeth
dulls it.

Your father robbed a Quik-Mart,
and the helicopters buzzed
around your vinegar neighborhood
for days. Your father was shot
in the right arm by a cop,
and you woke up the next morning
determined to become ambidextrous.

…in Greek, "nostalgia" means "the pain from an old wound"—

And I will tell you again: effective promises
are only made after cleaning vomit
out of a disintegrated living room carpet.
I was 11 and my sour hands became
my reflection: *I will never drink.*
I will never become my parents.

Now: my mother, 6 and a half
years sober. My father, gone but not
gone enough, still out there
buying two bottles of Charles Shaw
every Friday after work. Me, 21,
ordering a drink the week after
my birthday and believing
it will make me less desolate,
if only for the night.

Me, 21, apologizing to the child
covered in clotted baking soda.
The past life that was once
too present. The half-ghost
all this caution was born for.

I have invented so many porches
for us to fall in love on. I braved
the cold for you every time.
It was raining the only time we kissed.

Androphobia: the fear of men.
Theophobia: the fear of god.
Onomatophobia: the fear of names.
Hoplophobia: the fear of guns.
Genuphobia: the fear of knees.
Somniphobia: the fear of sleep.
Barophobia: the fear of gravity.
Catoptrophobia: the fear of mirrors.
Monophobia: the fear of being alone.
Nostophobia: the fear of returning home.

Jeff Mangum sang, *God is a place you will wait for the rest of your life*.

God is a place, and my father locked all the doors.
God is Vesuvius, the faults under San Francisco,
the riots on 4th Avenue after March Madness.

God is forgetting, and I'll shear my hair away
in the name of that savior.

I want you to study my shoulders:
the craters and the cherry pit scabs.

I feel so much more gruesome from behind,
13 years of my skin wreaking havoc

on itself, ouroboros unable to shed.
When I'm nervous my fingers find

new parts to destroy. That's half
the problem: I'm just as responsible

for the brutality as I'm not.

My grandparents traded Illinois for Arizona 7 years ago, but sometimes the mountains still fold in on themselves as we watch from their patio. They know your name, but still always call you *Himself*. My grandmother peels an orange: *will you see Himself again soon?* Every word out of my mouth fogs. I have told them too much about you, and they already love you.

Am I always going to live in places that catch on fire?

I'm not a woman
but
I'm still a teenage girl
watching herself weep
in the mirror, mimicking
Liepke paintings
when no one is looking.
I shed my sundress, watch
it turn to a puddle
of mollusk ink on the bedroom floor.

Wherever you are, whatever
you're doing—will your feet
be stained with my absence?

The command God gives the most
in the Bible: "do not be afraid."

In an airport diner, my father called me.
Neither of us knew it'd be the last time
we'd speak to each other. In their living room
in Minneapolis, a friend told me
to mourn him as if he'd died:

Wouldn't you say he's been dead
since before you were born?

In Boise, the phone company
emails me every month after
he pays his bill.

Look at all this country between us:
all the tundra, tornadoes, cowardice.
We once turned geography into the study
of loneliness, but I think by now we've made it
into the study of drifting. Eventually, it will be
again the study of the earth's physical form—
of a physicality beyond us. Listen:
this is what I sound like trying to remember
that this is what it means to love someone.

To keep quiet. To loosen your grip. To look
at the map and not see all the regret.

I start boxing classes.

I Google "Carthaginian peace."

I will not forgive my father, but I will forgive
the salt on my hands.

There's this recurring dream I've been having:
a farmhouse as old as this whole state.
Its paint falters into orange, then slowly withers
into dark batwing embers.

Nearby, all the iron melts. The trains
begin to wander aimlessly. The sky
shifts and resembles a mirror.

For what feels like the first time,
I unclench my jaw.

Once, my father caught me ripping
open a centimeter of my arm,

and he threatened to tie my hands
behind my back. *No boy will want you*

if you tear yourself apart like that.
Maybe he was right.

But I don't want the boys right back.

A DETERMINATION

My arm crowned in flowers nearly a year,
I choose to chase the joy again. After all,

I still believe that everything is full. Even
when my fridge starves itself again.

Even when I stain my best white blouse
with melted butter. This past summer,

Jade held my hand while the needle blazed
through my skin, letting go only to mimic

the drums on the radio above my head.
I cook spaghetti for Jade on my grease-dressed

stove, and she says *I think becoming
your friend is the best thing that's happened to me*

all year. After, I salt the pasta, add more water
to the pot, wrap my arms around her, realize

the feeling is mutual. This year is mutual.
Please understand, I beg myself:

the worst year of your life is still crowned
in flowers. Jade goes home; I empty

the clouded vase next to my bed. I wash my hands.
For a moment, the joy sticks to my skin like ice cubes.

GHOST STORY//
ORIGIN STORY

i.

David was the slingshot, but he never meant
to break the windows. He grew
to be over six feet tall. He always carried chewing tobacco,
and kept the clocks at military time. He wrote
most of a thousand page novel in a donut shop.
He was afraid of having children. When my grandmother
called to tell us my uncle was dead, she called me
by my mother's name: *Amy. Amy. Amy.*
Before that morning, I had wanted

to be mistaken for an adult so badly. My grandmother turned
every picture frame inside out. My grandfather
said: *I thought I saw my father at Meijer today,*
but it was just my own reflection in the frozen aisle.
My grandfather said: I thought I saw my son
at the rec center today, but it was only me. I was alone
in the room. The first time I tried to kill myself,
no one said his name. The first time I was published,

he was a monsoon of confetti in the dining room:
Another writer in the family. He would be so proud
of you. When my hair begins to tumble
at my shoulders the way his did, my grandmother
gathers it into a bouquet in her hands. I buy
round silver glasses, and she offers
to clean them for me every morning. My eyes

are hazel, just like her grief. She pours herself
into them: *he was born the day John Glenn*
orbited the earth, so of course every baby boy
in that hospital was named for him. But Jim
and I were stubborn about it, and we knew
he was always going to be David. David. David—

ii.

David was

        my uncle
  my

                        grandmother

said

he was

        me

I ONLY MISGENDER MYSELF WHEN FLEETWOOD MAC COMES ON

I'm not a woman, but part of me
is always going to be a teenage girl,
screaming into rivers and watching
herself weep in the mirror. Sometimes

> my hair grows like a curse word.
> My lipstick smears, and my teeth
> find a new hysteria.
> I still identify

as a spiteful bitch. The gold dust settles
on my cheeks, but I don't. The tables
have turned,

> and now my father is afraid of me.
> Damn my fury, damn my forgiveness.
> I've learned to fight like an anarchist racehorse—

my legs will give out before my heart does.
When I was still a girl, I cut all my hair

> in mourning. Twice. When I was still a girl,
> I found my grandmother's childhood braid
> framed in an attic. She sliced it off
> while angry at her father. I sleep

with scissors next to my bed, just in case.
I practice a running start. I tell the mirror
what I want to tell my father:

you will never get away from the sound
of the [   ] that hates you.

BRADLEY SAYS "YOU ARE LUCKY TO BE FROM SOMEWHERE"

& I know exactly what they mean: to watch your hometown
silver, & never consider gutting you. I'll bring
a dull knife to this fight, remember that poem all my teachers

asked me to write. Here's where I am, & here's where
I am again. I'm at my uncle's cobwebbed porch light,
& I'm at the wilting deer carcass by my father's trailer.

I'm at the saguaros, wishing I was taller & more sewing needle.
I'm at the hospital I was born in, replacing every window
with my mother's hands. I'm at the Snake River, my own hands

full of my grandfather's ashes. I'm at the Sertraline, a pebble
in my throat. I'm at the dirt on my boots, red blood cells
half-frozen & stargazing. Two years & a highway full

of phobias. Eight months & a new tube of lipstick
in my pocket. Six weeks & my grandfather's notebook
with only the words *palsy / ankle / appetite* tremored

into the first page. Yet still, I feel lucky. I do not flinch
when I tell someone this. It's all matter-of-fact, blunt
as a name. I trace myself back to the butchered beginning

with my own fingertips, and I say *thank you.* I say,
thank God. Perhaps the knowing is my city, the scuffs
on my sneakers. This isn't going to fit on the paperwork,

but it does fit on me. A dress of this fine a fabric,
& look: I have every occasion to wear it.

SOMEDAY I'LL LOVE LYD HAVENS

After Frank O'Hara / Roger Reeves / Ocean Vuong

Lyd, daydreaming of rewriting the etymology
isn't getting you anywhere. Your uncle
is still dead. You still are made from

your father. All the men who've put
their hands on you are slowly forgetting
your name, and yet you will always

remember theirs. Names are not
sheet-covered shadows. Not exorcisms,
not a knife's sunrise. Just look at your name:

shortened, but not dulled. That soft syllable
you love so dearly now. You love like
petrichor on the sidewalks, Lyd. Sometimes

you love like downpour too, but sometimes
that's a miracle. Where did you even learn
how to do that? You were born

into violence and you stripped it all away,
dirty clothes in front of a shower.
You do not have to forget; you shouldn't.

But remember to remember, Lyd. Turn
memory into a good luck charm. Rename
the dead flowers after yourself. Remind

the drought that it's not welcome here.

UNSAYINGS

In the postscript of that spiteful year,
I could only focus on where I was not.
Forgive me—*I was teething on roses,*

my mouth so bloody it became a bouquet
all its own. My womanless frame
wandered aimlessly from state-line
to state-line, avoiding eye contact

with everyone. This included the mirror.

The living room was overflowing
with bouquets, and everyone
kept apologizing to me almost as much
as I apologized to them. I'm sorry
I'm so quiet. My grandfather died
in that corner, and he never finished
the book I got him for Christmas.
I tried reading it to him while he drifted,
but every passage was about death.

I have my father's chest
and my mother's throat.
The scars on my back
never shut up. I always
hold the bottle cap
on the edge of my teeth
while I pour, my top lip
curled like a candle's wick.

Of course everything overflows.

What are we owed? Maybe the answers stain us.

Forgive me. I was tired of chairs
without backs. Of instant coffee
and telling hospice nurses who I am
without giving them my name.

My first gift to myself is the new year,
two hours early. In Florida, I wear
black velvet and drink apple cider
straight from the dancer-necked bottle.

The ball drops, and I laugh for ten minutes straight—
hysterical, and headstrong, and honey-dripped.

My friend TC says, "If your mind is a wasteland,
stillness is a rhythm."

Susan Orlean writes, "Sometimes I think
I've figured out some order in the universe,
but then I find myself in Florida."

In the December-January humidity
and the carnivorous leaves, I find
my new order. I stare the passage
of time in the face, and I stay
perfectly still.

Memory: the most unreliable part of the body.

Memory: a rope burn on my left wrist.

Memory: the garden in Illinois two strange boys
tore up. Or maybe they set it on fire. Or did they
just plant tulips?

I've never had a happy New Year,
just a deep exhale.

A howling wilderness. Two minutes before midnight.
A blank living room. Full of grace. The half-finished
obituary. Ten copies of the death certificate.

I can't decide if I believe in heaven,
but I absolutely believe in porches.
With the sun in my eyes, I watch
my mother chainsmoke. We repeat
for hours: we know he believed
there was nothing to look forward to
after death, and yet. We wonder
if he's just on a porch now,
easy and painless in a rocking chair.
The sun could be in his eyes too,
but he wouldn't feel a thing.

I still haven't made peace
with any of the men,
brutal or benign. Every *C*
my fingernails embroider
into my palms stands for *conflagration.*
My sunburns always peel
into momentary forgetting.

The dying dream about the dead—death,
a family reunion. I sat at my grandfather's bedside
and held my breath. He opened his eyes.
Looked to me. Said, *son.* Wide as horizons
before he slipped back into quiet.

My mirror: permanently frozen
with a dead man's reflection.
My blessing, my curse.

I am still learning how to celebrate
with bittersweetness in my mouth.
I am still learning how to look
in the mirror and say *thank you.*

When the cardinal was tattooed
into my left arm, my angry skin
gave him his red wings.

When I covered the sight
of every grief with my hands,
the sky paled and dissolved
into humming.

A new year might not be truly new,
but I'm still soaking myself
in the sugar of it. I wear my longest
earrings and sharpest eyeliner.
I sing "Dancing in the Dark"
at the karaoke bar and laugh
into Emily's shoulder. Being alive

is noisy business, but even the softer songs
are filling. If I don't start singing now,
I'll never get around to it.

More often than I wish to admit,
I mix up the words *palinode* and *palindrome*—

my unsayings are always the same
backward and forward.

Let me tell this story one more time:

the temperature wouldn't drop
below 113. I kept returning
to the front yard. I kept dreaming
about eating dirt. My grandfather
has now been dead for six months.
The last words I ever said to him were *I love you,*
I'll see you soon. His hand rubber in mine.

A few hours later, his mouth began to turn purple.

I have my uncle's brown eyes
and petunia-shaped mouth.
His taste in movies and penchant
for cured meats. When he died,
everyone stared at my face
so longingly I started to cry.

My grandfather's last word to me
was *son.* I choose to believe
he was asking for sunlight.

MY GRANDMOTHER, IN MAINE AT DAWN

after Franz Wright

Your father tried to tell you he won the war
all by himself. You told me this decades later
with red contempt in your face. My great-grandfather,
born a whole century before me, became my worst enemy.
The way my father was my worst enemy. The way
he was also yours. What a lineage you drew for us:

little girls who remind men of the death
wishes on their backs. A circle we wear
on our middle fingers again and again. I was eight
the first time I saw the state you came from,
and understood why your mouth said the letter *O*
like the letter *u*. From the farmhouse, I watched

as you finished your morning walk, the sunrise
catching your halo of gnats. Your hair, bright
and indescribable. I remembered the photos of you
as a child, your hair like corn silk and soil
outlining your hands. Even with your back
to the camera, I can tell when you're smiling.
Sweet blueberry girl with a namesake and a half,
causing trouble for over 80 years. I promise
to remember.

Notes & Gratitudes

My gratitude is owed to the journals that first published these poems:

Tinderbox Poetry Journal: "XX"
Pretty Owl Poetry: "Chokecherry," "Maine Laments"
Foglifter: "206 days later"
Glass, a Journal of Poetry: "Notname"
The Shallow Ends: "Elegy ending in my grandmother remembering"
Flypaper Lit: "I only misgender myself when Fleetwood Mac comes on"

———

"Notname" references a painting of Elizabeth I that is now typically attributed to William Scrots.

"Boomtown (all the places I am not)" shares its title with the painting "Boomtown" by Patrick Kilby, exhibited in the Idaho State Museum. The first section is also inspired by the painting. It also quotes the first season finale of *Mad Men* and "Two-Headed Boy (Pt. 2)" by Neutral Milk Hotel.

"A determination" is about and for Jade Browne.

"I only misgender myself when Fleetwood Mac comes on" references lines from Fleetwood Mac's songs "The Chain," "Gold Dust Woman," and "Silver Springs."

The title "Bradley says you are lucky to be from somewhere" references something Bradley Trumpfheller told me in July of 2018.

"Unsayings" borrows a line from "Humiliation" by The National; it also quotes "Dystopia: Dancefloor" by TC Kody and *The Orchid Thief* by Susan Orlean.

This book, first and foremost, is for my uncle David and my grandparents, Sally and Jim. The grief of losing you was so strong I had to write a whole book about it, all because of how brilliant and beautiful you were. I would not be here without you three, period. Thank you for everything. I love you, I love you, I love you.

I could not imagine finding a warmer home for this book than Game Over Books. Thank you, Josh, for telling me I should send it, and for taking such great care of it. Thank you to the entire GOB team: Kaleigh, Liv, Dena, MJ, Story, Jillian. I am constantly in awe of you, and of all the authors I'm lucky enough to be published alongside.

Thank you to my professors and mentors, especially Emily Pittinos, Katie Fuller, Kerri Webster, Tessy Ward, Sam McPhee, and Emily Ruskovich. This book would not be as sharp and intentional without your guidance and support. Nor would I. My writing owes you its life.

There were moments in the year 2020, the year of the Biggest Griefs, that I wasn't sure I'd make it, but Jade Browne helped me pull myself through. Thank you, Jade, again and again. Having you as a best friend has been one of the greatest gifts of all.

Thank you to my Beachie Boys, K Lange and Emily Ruth Herbster. You showed me how much joy is worth sticking around for. You carried me home, and you showed me what home is.

Thank you to many other friends who have lit my life up: Dorothy, TC, Paige, Joplin, Noah, Kate Wilson, Wheeler, Devin, Catherine, Desireé, Matador, Cay, Topaz, Percy, Truj, Arianna Monet, Myles, Lip, Red, and so many more. Thank you as well to Dave, Mary, and Sara Mae for your beautiful blurbs—what an honor and a treasure it is to be seen by people I admire so much.

There are so many poets, artists and genuinely wonderful beings in Boise that continuously inspire me. I am especially indebted to Cheryl Maddalena, Tara and Ben Lzicar, Risë Kevalshar Collins, Alfredo Ocaranza González, Jacob Robarts, Caitlin McGowan, Noel Nelson, and Lianne Collins. I am constantly inspired by your community, craft, love and support.

I am so lucky to have such a loving and supportive family. My deepest thanks are owed to my mother—everything I do and write is for you, and is my best attempt at saying thank you. Thank you to Ken and Max, as well as Karen, Bertie, Neil, Heather, Daniel, Maddie, Sami, Jack, Kris, and all the Wallaces and Fosters. Our love for one another has gotten us through some deep griefs, and I don't take that for granted for even a second. I love you.

Thank you, reader. There was a time in my life when I didn't think anybody would ever care to read whatever I had to say. Thank you, wherever you are, for proving me wrong. Thank you for being here.

Lyd Havens is a reader and writer currently living in Boise, Idaho. Their work has previously been published in *Ploughshares, Poetry Northwest, The Shallow Ends,* and *Tinderbox Poetry Journal,* among others. They are the author of *I Gave Birth to All the Ghosts Here* (Nostrovia! Press, 2018), and the winner of the 2018 ellipsis… Poetry Prize. Lyd will graduate with a BFA in Creative Writing from Boise State University in the fall of 2021.